AF288620

Laws

Who Needs Them and How They Work

Materialien für den bilingualen Unterricht: Politik
Laws – Who Needs Them and How They Work

Erarbeitet von
Annegret Weeke und Johannes Zieger

Redaktion: Merlene Griffin, Marc Proulx (verantwortlich)
Umschlaggestaltung: Klein & Halm Grafikdesign, Berlin
Layoutkonzept: werkstatt für gebrauchsgrafik, Berlin
Technische Umsetzung: Heike Freund, Hameln

www.cornelsen.de

Die Webseiten Dritter, deren Internetadressen in diesem Lehrwerk angegeben sind,
wurden vor Drucklegung sorgfältig geprüft. Der Verlag übernimmt keine Gewähr für
die Aktualität und den Inhalt dieser Seiten oder solcher, die mit ihnen verlinkt sind.

1. Auflage, 6. Druck 2023

Alle Drucke dieser Auflage sind inhaltlich unverändert
und können im Unterricht nebeneinander verwendet werden.

Druck: Esser printSolutions GmbH, Bretten

ISBN 978-3-464-31099-1

PEFC-zertifiziert
Dieses Produkt
stammt aus
nachhaltig
bewirtschafteten
Wäldern und
kontrollierten Quellen
PEFC/04-31-2851   www.pefc.de

Preface

Laws – Who Needs Them and How They Work is a bilingual module for use in your politics class. It looks at questions and issues concerning the purpose of laws, the effect they have on our lives and the consequences of breaking them. In this module you will find the following elements:

Texts

which give you an overview of or introduce you to the subject. Words with an asterisk* are important political terms which are explained in the Glossary of terms (see the Appendix, p. 16).

Figures

for you to work with: statistics, diagrams, and photos. They are labelled with an 'F' and are numbered throughout the module.

Skills boxes

give you strategies and tools for working with the tasks and analysing the different kinds of sources.

Key terms

These boxes give you further information on important terms used in the module. Marked in bold, they are useful for your revision of the topic.

F 8 Who's who in a German criminal court

Key terms

Sentence
In criminal cases, if a defendant is found guilty of¹ a crime, he or she is given a sentence, i.e. the judge decides² in court what particular punishment the criminal will get.

She was given an 18-month prison sentence.
As a verb: He was sentenced³ to 18 months in prison.

New vocabulary

All numbered words are explained or translated on the same page.

Tasks

In each section you will find different kinds of tasks which help you to understand a development or issue, for example

– by **organizing information** in charts and diagrams to simplify and summarize information, making it easier to understand and remember.
– by **making connections**: tasks in which you think critically about problems, draw comparisons or think about the effect that laws have on your life.
– by **doing extra research**: tasks that tell you to research a topic further, on the Internet or using other reference material.

Activate your English

These boxes provide you with words and phrases for writing and speaking about the topics which are dealt with in the tasks.

Activate your English

Talking about causes and effects

because of sth.	wegen etwas
the reason for this / why	der Grund dafür/, warum
have the effect that	die Wirkung/Effekt haben, dass
lead-led-led to sth.	führen zu etwas
the longer, the …	je länger, desto …
the easier, the …	je einfacher, desto …
as a result/consequence	folglich

Module revision

At the end of the module there are activities which help you revise key terms and vocabulary and make you think further about the main issues of the module.

Appendix

In the Appendix you will find a glossary of political terms and an English-German vocabulary list with translations of the key terms in the module. These features will help make the reading in this module easier and more enjoyable for you. A German-English vocabulary list will help you find words and phrases for use in your written tasks and discussions.

Laws

Who Needs Them and How They Work

1 What are laws?

F 1 A police officer checks the speed[1] of traffic with a speed gun[2]

1 speed (n) *Geschwindig-keit*

2 speed gun *Geschwindig-keitsmesser*

3 citizen *Bürger/in*

4 enforce the law *das Gesetz durchsetzen*

5 break – broke – broken the law *gegen das Gesetz verstoßen*

6 traffic warden *Politesse*

7 crime *Verbrechen*

8 suspect *Verdächtige(r)*

9 court *Gericht*

10 punish sb./sth. *jdn./etwas bestrafen*

11 elect sb. *jdn. wählen*

12 representative *Vertreter/in*

13 protect sb./sth. (from sb./sth.) *jdn./etwas (vor jdm./etwas) schützen*

14 treat sb./sth. unfairly *jdn./etwas ungerecht behandeln*

15 create order *Ordnung schaffen*

Every country has its own set of laws or rules that help people live together without conflict. Every citizen[3] must follow these laws and everyone is equal before the law. Many different people enforce the law[4], i.e. make sure that the law is not broken[5]:
- Traffic wardens[6] look after parking.
- Health inspectors check that the food in restaurants is clean.
- The police arrest crime[7] suspects[8].
- Courts[9] punish[10] lawbreakers.

In Germany the people elect[11] their representatives[12] to parliament (*Bundestag* and *Bundesrat*), which then makes laws for the people. However, laws are now being made more and more often by the European Union*. This is to make sure that they are the same in all 27 member states. For example, European law says that the water on European beaches must be tested regularly.

Why we need laws
Laws are made to:
- protect[13] people so that they do not get hurt
- protect people so that they are not treated[14] unfairly
- create order[15]
- teach people the difference between right and wrong.

An example of a law

Jugendarbeitsschutzgesetz[1] (JArbSchG)

(1) Kind im Sinne dieses Gesetzes ist, wer noch nicht 15 Jahre alt ist.
(2) Jugendlicher im Sinne dieses Gesetzes ist, wer 15, aber noch nicht 18 Jahre alt ist.

Dieses Gesetz gilt nicht
1. für geringfügige Hilfeleistungen, soweit sie gelegentlich aus Gefälligkeit erbracht werden,
2. für die Beschäftigung im Familienhaushalt.

Beschäftigung von Kindern
(1) Die Beschäftigung von Kindern (§ 2 Abs. 1) ist verboten.
(2) Das Verbot des Absatzes 1 gilt nicht für die Beschäftigung von Kindern im Rahmen des Betriebspraktikums während der Vollzeitschulpflicht.
(3) Das Verbot des Absatzes 1 gilt ferner nicht für die Beschäftigung von Kindern über 13 Jahre mit Einwilligung der Eltern, soweit die Beschäftigung leicht und für Kinder geeignet ist. Die Beschäftigung ist leicht, wenn sie auf Grund ihrer Beschaffenheit und der besonderen Bedingungen, unter denen sie ausgeführt wird,
1. die Sicherheit, Gesundheit und Entwicklung der Kinder,
2. ihren Schulbesuch, ihre Beteiligung an Maßnahmen zur Berufswahlvorbereitung oder Berufsausbildung, die von der zuständigen Stelle anerkannt sind, und
3. ihre Fähigkeit, dem Unterricht mit Nutzen zu folgen, nicht nachteilig beeinflusst. Die Kinder dürfen nicht mehr als zwei Stunden täglich, in landwirtschaftlichen Familienbetrieben nicht mehr als drei Stunden täglich, nicht zwischen 18 und 8 Uhr, nicht vor dem Schulunterricht und nicht während des Schulunterrichts beschäftigt werden.
(4) Das Verbot des Absatzes 1 gilt ferner nicht für die Beschäftigung von Jugendlichen während der Schulferien für höchstens vier Wochen im Kalenderjahr.

F2 Child labour in India

1 **a** Point out which laws the police officer is trying to enforce in F1 (p. 4) and what aim she is trying to achieve[2].
   b Imagine you are the driver in F1 and realize that your speed is being checked. Write down what you might be thinking or feeling.
2 Look at the list of reasons for making laws at the bottom of p. 4. Which of the reasons do you find most important? Discuss with a partner.
3 Does the *Jugendarbeitsschutzgesetz* allow
   a your parents to tell you to go shopping for your family?
   b you to work in your parents' restaurant on Saturday evenings?
   c your 11-year-old brother to do the paper-round[3]?
   d you to work during your summer holidays?
   Justify[4] your answers. (Language help: *Because the law states[5] that … / children are allowed[6] to … / children are not allowed to … / … is forbidden.*)
4 Explain in your own words why this law was made and why it is important.

1 Jugendarbeitsschutz-gesetz *The Protection of Young Persons Employment Act*
2 achieve an aim *ein Ziel erreichen*
3 do the paper-round *Zeitungen austragen*
4 justify sth. *etwas rechtfertigen*
5 state *feststellen, sagen*
6 be allowed to do sth. *etwas tun dürfen*

5 Not all countries have laws that protect young children from having to start work at an early age (see F2, p. 5). Imagine how your life would change if you lived in such a country as the child of poor parents. Draw a cause-and-effect diagram[1] to show how that situation would affect[2] you and your future (see the Skills box below).

6 Even in countries where laws protecting young children do exist, they are often not respected. Think of possible reasons people might have for breaking these laws, then demonstrate your findings in a type-3 cause-and-effect diagram (see below).

Skills box

Making a cause-and-effect diagram

A cause-and-effect diagram is useful for showing what consequences (effects[3]) an action (cause[4]) may have.

Type 1: A cause may have an effect which then becomes the cause for another effect.

Cause	Effect
Higher taxes on petrol[5] ⟶	higher petrol prices
Higher petrol prices ⟶	?

Type 2: One cause may have many effects.

	…
Smoking is banned[6] in restaurants ⟶	…
	…

Type 3: Many causes can lead to the same effect.

…	
…	⟶ The **Jugendarbeitsschutzgesetz** (Protection of Young Persons Employment Act) is not respected.
…	

Activate your English

Talking about causes and effects

because of sth.	wegen etwas
the reason for this / why	der Grund dafür/, warum
have the effect that	die Wirkung/Effekt haben, dass
lead-led-led to sth.	führen zu etwas
the longer, the …	je länger, desto …
the easier, the …	je einfacher, desto …
as a result/consequence	folglich

1 cause-and-effect diagram *Ursache-Wirkungs-Schema*

2 affect sb./sth. *auf jdn./etwas auswirken*

3 effect *Wirkung, Auswirkung*

4 cause *Ursache*

5 petrol *Benzin*

6 ban sth. *etwas verbieten*

2 How are our daily lives affected by laws and regulations*?

F3 Laws in daily life

Everyday activities	How they are affected by laws
The alarm clock wakes you up.	The time is set by law[1].
You take a shower.	We have laws that regulate how clean water must be.
You get dressed.	Clothing must have passed tests (e.g. it must have care instructions[2]).
You eat breakfast and brush your teeth.	The contents of toothpaste and food must be listed on the packaging[3].
You go to school.	The law does not only state that you must go to school, but also which subjects you take and for how long.
You are in the school building.	Buildings must have passed safety tests.
You travel home from school.	?
You phone a friend.	?
You watch TV.	?

The influence[4] of laws

Laws have been made that
- raise[5] the tax* on petrol (tax money is used for road repairs)
- ban smoking in restaurants
- demand[6] installation of air-pollution filters[7] in old cars
- forbid firemen and policemen to strike
- demand that all new medicines be tested before they can be sold
- limit the amount of[8] sugar in your breakfast cereal[9]
- protect the copyright[10] of films and music with licences[11]
- raise the fines[12] for speeding[13].

1 a Copy and complete the last three lines of the table in F3.
   b Choose three activities from the table and discuss why they are regulated by laws.
2 a In class, brainstorm why the laws in the list above were made and how they influence your life. (Language help: *The law which regulates/demands/forbids/raises … was made to … / makes it difficult/easier/possible for me/people to … / makes sure that …*)
   b Present your results in a table.
3 a Make two type-1 cause-and-effect diagrams (see the Skills box, p. 6) to show how two of the laws in the list above influence your life.
   b Choose one of the laws above and draw a type-2 cause-and-effect diagram to demonstrate the different possible effects this law can have.
   c Present your results to the class using the expressions in the **Activate your English** box on p. 6.

1 by law *gesetzlich geregelt*
2 care instructions *Pflegehinweis*
3 packaging (n) *Verpackung*
4 influence (n) *Einfluss*
5 raise sth. *etwas erhöhen*
6 demand sth. *etwas verlangen, fordern*
7 air-pollution filter *Rußpartikelfilter*
8 amount of *Menge an*
9 cereal *Müsli*
10 copyright *Urheberrecht*
11 licence *Lizenz*
12 fine *Strafgebühr, Bußgeld*
13 speeding (n) *Geschwindigkeitsüberschreitung*

3 Consequences of breaking the law

Max the shoplifter

Max M. (18) has a new girlfriend. He is very much in love and it is her birthday soon. He wants to surprise her with a nice T-shirt that she really likes, but it is too expensive for him. He does not want her to know that he cannot afford[1] it, but he does not want to give her anything cheap for her special day either. So for the first time in his life, in a moment of weakness, he slips the nice and expensive T-shirt into his pocket. He knows it is wrong, but he sees no other way.

The shop assistant, Ms Bauer, has been watching him for a while. She sees him putting something into his pocket and runs over and tells him that she has seen everything. When Max says he has not done anything wrong, Ms Bauer decides to call the police because only they are allowed to search[2] the boy's pockets. The police arrive and find the T-shirt in Max's

pocket. They inform Max that the shop owner will file a police report[3] against him for shoplifting[4]*, that he will hear from the public prosecutor[5]* and that he can expect a trial[6]. The owner of the shop also tells Max that he wants compensation[7] for the stolen T-shirt. 'I'll see you in court!,' he says. For the first time in his life, Max is in real trouble.

1 be able to afford sth. *sich etwas leisten können*
2 search sb./sth. *jdn./etwas durchsuchen*
3 file a police report against sb. *eine Anzeige gegen jdn. erstatten*
4 shoplifting *Ladendiebstahl*
5 public prosecutor *Staatsanwalt/-anwältin*
6 trial *Gerichtsverhandlung*
7 compensation *Schadenersatz, Entschädigung*
8 reported shoplifting cases *erfasste Ladendiebstähle*
9 harm sb./sth. *jdn./etwas verletzen, jdm. Schaden zufügen*
10 suffer damages *Schaden erleiden*

F4 Number of reported shoplifting cases[8] in Germany between 1997 and 2006. Experts believe that about 90% of cases are unreported.

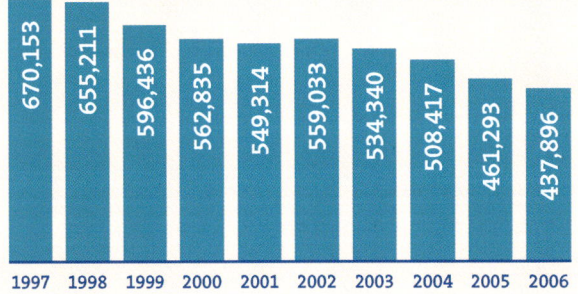

1997	1998	1999	2000	2001	2002	2003	2004	2005	2006
670,153	655,211	596,436	562,835	549,314	559,033	534,340	508,417	461,293	437,896

Source: Polizeiliche Kriminalstatistik, 2006

Activate your English

Talking about trends
between ... and ...
the number of ...
    went down / decreased /
    dropped / fell
    steadily/gradually/slowly/
    steeply/sharply
from (around) ... to (about)
    ... / by approximately ...%

1 Read Max's story again. Describe the rules and laws which have been broken. Has anybody been harmed[9] or suffered damages[10]*? Explain.

2 Discuss why the government / the people might be interested in punishing Max.

3 Look at F4. Describe and discuss the trends in shoplifting between 1997 and 2006. Give possible reasons for these trends and for the fact that most shoplifting cases are not reported. For language help, see the **Activate your English** box above.

Let the court decide ... but which one?

F5 Characteristics of criminal and civil courts

Criminal court[1]	*Civil court*[5]

• *The government / the people use the criminal court to punish individuals who have broken the law of a country.*
 • *The people want to protect themselves against those who do wrong.*
 • *A case in a criminal court is called a criminal case*[2]*.*
 • *Typical cases:*
  • *Stealing*
  • *Damaging*[3] *other people's property*[4]
  • *Taking illegal drugs*
	• *Citizens/businesses/companies use the civil court to help them solve*[6] *problems they have with each other.*
	 • *Usually people claim*[7] *money damages*[8] *or some other form of compensation.*
	 • *A case in a civil court is called a civil case*[9]*.*
	 • *Typical cases:*
	  • *Problems buying and selling goods*
	  • *Problems renting a flat*
	  • *Conflicts between neighbours*
	  • *Conflicts in the workplace*

Differences between civil cases and criminal cases
- In a criminal case a prosecutor, not the crime victim*, begins the case even if[10] the victim does not want this.
- In a civil case the injured party[11] is the one who starts the case.
- In a criminal case, if the accused[12]* is found guilty, they pay a fine[13], go to prison or both.
- People who lose civil cases may have to pay money damages, but they do not go to prison.
- In a criminal case a government-paid lawyer[14] represents[15] a defendant[16]* who wants a lawyer but cannot pay one.
- People in civil cases have to represent themselves or pay for their own lawyers.

1 Organize the above information into a table.
2 Will the cases below go to a criminal court, a civil court or both? Copy and complete the table.

Criminal court	Civil court	Both

- Shoplifting in a clothes shop
- Stealing a bike at school
- Driving without a driving licence[17]
- Selling illegally downloaded music files to your friends
- Painting graffiti on a shop
- Faking[18] the date on a train ticket
- Setting a rubbish bin on fire
- Driving a motorbike without a helmet
- Scratching[19] a car with your bike

1 criminal court *Straf-gericht*
2 criminal case *Strafsache*
3 damage sth. *etwas beschädigen*
4 property *Eigentum*
5 civil court *Zivilgericht*
6 solve sth. *etwas lösen, erlösen*
7 claim sth. *etwas beanspruchen, fordern*
8 damages (pl) *Schaden-ersatz*
9 civil case *Zivilsache*
10 even if *selbst wenn*
11 injured party *Geschädigte(r)*
12 accused *Angeklagte(r)*
13 pay a fine *eine Strafe bezahlen*
14 lawyer *Anwalt/Anwältin*
15 represent sb./sth. *jdn./etwas vertreten*
16 defendant *Beklagte(r)*
17 driving licence *Führerschein*
18 fake sth. *etwas fälschen*
19 scratch sb./sth. *jdn./etwas zerkratzen*

F6 Stages in a criminal case in Germany

Suspect

1st stage:
A person is suspected[1] of committing a crime[2].

2nd stage:
The police and the prosecutor begin investigations[3] and search for evidence[4]*.

3rd stage:
The prosecutor decides if there is enough evidence against the suspect.

4th stage:
If not, the charges are dropped[5].
If so, the public prosecutor charges[6] the suspect with a crime.

5th stage:
The judge* decides whether or not to begin the case.

5th stage:

Lay judge[7]*   Judge   Lay judge

Trial

Accused   **Defence counsel[8]***   **Prosecutor**

Verdict[9]

F7 Stages in a civil case in Germany

Civil cases begin when the injured party files a complaint[10] in court saying what problem they have with another person, company or organization and how they want it solved (for example, Paul has sprayed graffiti on the Schmidts' house and they want compensation for cleaning the walls). Lawyers are not necessary in a civil case. The defendant then files their statement. Both parties[11] have to give evidence for their statements. The judge may question[12] witnesses and experts. At the end of the case, the judge decides what each party has to do, the amount of money that must be paid to the person who wins their case, and who must pay the costs of the trial.

1 suspect sb. of sth. *jdn. einer Sache verdächtigen*
2 commit a crime *ein Verbrechen begehen*
3 investigation *Untersuchung*
4 evidence *Beweis*
5 drop the charges *die Anklage fallenlassen*
6 charge sb. with sth. *jdn. einer Sache anklagen*
7 lay judge *ehrenamtliche(r) Richter/in, Schöffe*
8 defence counsel *Verteidiger/in*
9 verdict *Urteilsspruch, Gerichtsurteil*
10 file a complaint *eine Klageschrift einreichen*
11 party *Partei*
12 question sb. *jdn. befragen, verhören*
13 flow chart *Flussdiagramm*

1 Imagine you are the lawyer representing Max in court. Using the diagram in F6 above, inform Max about what is going to happen in his case – what the police, the prosecutor and the judge will do.

2 Explain why both the prosecutor and the judge examine the evidence before they decide to begin the case.

3 Design a flow chart[13] (see F6 and also the Appendix, p. 16) showing the different stages in a civil case (see F7 above).

Who's who in court?

Prosecutor

I am the lawyer on the government's side in criminal trials. I charge the suspect and try to prove[1] that the accused is guilty[2].

Defence counsel

I am the lawyer who represents the accused person in a criminal case. I try to prove that the accused is not guilty.

Accused

The prosecutor has charged me with committing a crime and will try to prove that I did it. I have the right to be in court to hear everything that happens in my case.

Victim of the crime

I have suffered[3] physically or emotionally as the result of a crime. My property was damaged. I appear in court as a witness[4]*.

Witness

I am called to court to give evidence. This means I come to court to talk about what I have seen or heard.

I am only allowed to give evidence about my own personal experiences[5], i.e. what I saw, heard, said, felt or smelled. On the day that I give evidence, I must wait outside the courtroom until my name is called. In the witness box[6]*, I am sometimes asked to swear an oath[7] to tell the truth[8]. I have the right to remain silent[9] if the accused is a close relative[10].

Lay judge

I listen to the evidence in criminal cases where the maximum prison sentence[11]* is not higher than four years. Together with the judge, two lay judges decide whether the accused is guilty or not guilty. If the accused is declared guilty[12], we decide together what sentence they should get. In Germany any German citizen with no criminal record[13] can become a lay judge. As a lay judge you do not need professional knowledge about law, just common sense[14]. In contrast to the judge, defence counsel and public prosecutor, I do not have to wear a robe[15].

Plaintiff[16]* and defendant

We are the two parties in a civil case. We can be one person, a group of people, an organization or a business. The plaintiff is the person or group who is suing[17]. The defendant is the party being sued. We can both have lawyers to represent us.

1 prove sth. *etwas beweisen*
2 guilty *schuldig*
3 suffer *leiden*
4 witness *Zeuge/Zeugin*
5 experience *Erfahrung*
6 witness box *Zeugenbank*
7 swear an oath *einen Eid ablegen*
8 tell the truth *die Wahrheit sagen*
9 remain silent *schweigen*
10 relative *Verwandte(r)*
11 sentence (n) *Urteil, Strafmaß*
12 declare sb. guilty *jdn. für schuldig erklären*
13 have a criminal record *vorbestraft sein*
14 common sense *gesunder Menschenverstand*
15 robe *Talar*
16 plaintiff *Zivilkläger/in*
17 sue sb. for sth. *jdn. wegen etwas verklagen, etwas von jdm. einklagen*

The public

We are allowed to sit in the public gallery[1] of the courtroom to watch the case. In certain cases, however, the judge decides that the court should be closed. If so, only the lawyers, the accused, the witnesses and people directly involved[2] in the case can stay in the courtroom. The court can also be closed when a child gives evidence.

Judge

I hear civil or criminal cases. When I enter the courtroom everybody has to stand up. Together with the lay judges I decide on the sentence in criminal cases. In civil cases I decide what the plaintiff and defendant have to do or the amount of money that must be paid to someone for winning their case.

Key terms

Sentence

In criminal cases, if a defendant is found guilty of[3] a crime, they are given a sentence, i.e. the judge decides[4] in court what particular punishment the criminal will get.

She was given an 18-month prison sentence.
As a verb: *He was sentenced[5] to 18 months in prison.*

According to German law, the possible sentences for shoplifting are as follows:

§ 242 StGB [Diebstahl]

(1) Wer eine fremde bewegliche Sache einem anderen in der Absicht wegnimmt, die Sache sich oder einem Dritten rechtswidrig zuzueignen, wird mit Freiheitsstrafe bis zu fünf Jahren oder mit Geldstrafe bestraft.
(2) Der Versuch ist strafbar.

§ 248a StGB Diebstahl und Unterschlagung geringwertiger Sachen

Der Diebstahl und die Unterschlagung geringwertiger Sachen werden gemäß § 248a StGB nur auf Antrag verfolgt. (Antragsdelikt)
Als geringwertig wird eine Sache mit einem Wert von maximal 35 € anzusehen sein.
Beim Ladendiebstahl wird regelmäßig Strafantrag durch den geschädigten Ladenbesitzer oder die beauftragte Detektei gestellt.

As a rule, shop owners file a police report against shoplifters.

1 public gallery
  Zuschauergalerie
2 be involved in sth. *an etwas beteiligt sein*
3 be found guilty of sth. *einer Sache für schuldig befunden werden*
4 decide sth. *sich (für etwas) entscheiden*
5 sentence sb. to sth. (v) *jdn. zu etwas verurteilen*

1 Who does what? Match the person to the correct description.

1.	The prosecutor ...	**a)**	sits in the public gallery of the courtroom.
2.	The public ...	**b)**	talks about what they have seen and heard.
3.	The victim of the crime ...	**c)**	sues somebody because they believe that this person is responsible for damaging their property.
4.	The lay judge ...	**d)**	listens to the witnesses and the evidence and decides on the verdict and possible sentence.
5.	The defence counsel ...	**e)**	is sued because somebody believes that they are responsible for damaging their her property.
6.	The plaintiff ...	**f)**	charges somebody with a crime.
7.	The accused ...	**g)**	has suffered because of a crime.
8.	The judge ...	**h)**	represents the accused.
9.	The witness ...	**i)**	hears the trial and decides with the judge whether the defendant is guilty or not guilty.
10.	The defendant ...	**j)**	is charged with a crime and may be punished.

2 a 'Who am I?': Choose one of the people above. Describe yourself to a partner in just three sentences. Your partner must guess who you are and then introduce you to the class.
  b Translate sentences 1–10 above into German and compare your results in class.
3 Imagine you are talking to English-speaking friends about the system of law in Germany. Explain to them what punishment they should expect if they shoplift in Germany.

F 8   **Who's who in a German criminal court**

4 Who's who? Look at F8 above.
  a In your exercise books, write down in English who or what each number represents.
  b Give possible reasons why some of the people mentioned in 'Who's who in court' (pp. 11–12) are not included in the illustration.

5 Fill in the missing steps in Max's trial using the sentences in the boxes below.

Steps in the trial

1.	…
2.	The prosecutor reads out the charges[1].
3.	…
4.	The court clerk[2]* calls the witness (the shop assistant).
5.	…
6.	The defence counsel questions the shop assistant.
7.	…
8.	The court clerk calls the accused, Max, to the witness box and asks him to tell the truth.
9.	…
10.	The prosecutor questions Max.
11.	…
12.	…
13.	The defence counsel gives a closing speech[3]. They explain that …
14.	Together with the lay judges, the judge decides if Max is (a) guilty or (b) not guilty **a)** **b)** If Max is not found guilty of the crime, he goes free[4].

> The defence counsel pleads guilty[5] or not guilty.

> The defence counsel questions Max.

> The prosecutor questions the shop assistant and tries to find out all the facts. They try to prove that the accused committed the crime of shoplifting.

> The prosecutor demands Max's conviction[6] in their closing speech.

> The judge allows the boy to leave the witness box.

> The judge opens the case.

> The judge allows the shop assistant, Ms Bauer, to leave the witness box.

> If Max is found guilty of the crime, the judge sentences him and explains why this sentence is fair.

1 charge *Anklage*

2 court clerk *Gerichts-diener/in*

3 closing speech *Schlussplädoyer (die zusammenfassende Schlussrede des Staatsanwalts und des Verteidigers)*

4 go free *freikommen*

5 plead guilty *sich schuldig bekennen*

6 conviction *Verurteilung*

6 Imagine you are Max's defence counsel.
   a Write down the questions you would ask him in the witness box in order to help him.
   b Write your closing speech. How would you explain what happened?

7 Find all the matching verbs in this module for
   • what the different people do
     e.g. *The judge decides/questions … / the prosecutor … / the police …*
   • what you can do with the law or what the law does.
     e.g. *break the law / the law states that …*

Module revision

Laws – Who Needs Them and How They Work

Key terms

civil court, criminal court, judge, prosecutor, defence counsel, accused, defendant, plaintiff, witness, sentence, lay judge

Skills

Making a cause-and-effect diagram, p. 6

Activate your English

Talking about causes and effects, p. 6
Talking about trends, p. 8

1 Using the shoplifting incident, write down who's who in a civil and criminal court.
2 Are there lay judges in Max's case? Explain your answer.
3 Are these statements true or false? Write the corrected answers into your exercise book.
  a Children under the age of 15 are not allowed to work in the family household[1].
  b A 14 year old may work on the fields in a family farm, but not any more than three hours per day.
  c Witnesses must tell the truth if they are under oath[2].
  d Witnesses have to tell the court everything they know even if the accused is a close relative.
  e If someone does something wrong, they can only be tried[3] once, either in a civil or in a criminal court.
  f A trial is always public. Only cases involving children and cases of domestic violence[4] are often closed to the public.
4 Point out the advantages of a public trial.
5 Paul calls himself a graffiti artist, but the police have arrested him for damaging public and private property several times. As Paul's lawyer, tell him what he should expect.
6 Don't say it!
Step 1: Form groups of three and write the following terms on separate index cards: criminal court, civil court, prosecutor, defence counsel, accused, witness, lay judge, plaintiff, defendant, judge, witness box, law, closing speech.
Step 2: Write five words on each index card to describe the term. Give all of your index cards to your teacher.
Step 3: Your teacher will now give each of you an index card. You must explain the term to your class without saying the words written on the card. The rest of the class must note down how many sentences you need to explain the term before they guess what it is.

1 household *Haushalt*
2 under oath *unter Eid*
3 try – tried – tried sb. *jdn. vor Gericht stellen*
4 domestic violence *häusliche Gewalt*

Glossary of terms

accused: the person or party brought to court for committing a crime. See also p. 11.

civil case: a type of court case that takes places in a civil court to help people solve problems they have with one another. See also p. 9.

court clerk: an official in charge of the records of the court.

crime victim: a person who has suffered because of a crime. See also p. 11.

criminal case: a type of court case in which a person who has broken the law is given a punishment. It takes place in a criminal court. See also p. 9.

damages: the amount of money that a court decides should be paid to a person, group or organization by the party that has caused them harm or injury.

defence counsel: a lawyer who represents the defendant and tries to prove in court that they did not commit a crime. See also p. 11.

defendant: a person who is accused of committing a crime (in a criminal case) or who is being sued (in a civil case). See also p. 11.

evidence: information given in court to try to prove sth.

European Union: an economic and political organization made up of 27 European countries.

judge: a person in court who has the authority to decide what punishment criminals should get, or to make legal decisions. See also p. 12.

lay judge: a person who listens to evidence in a court case and decides, along with the judge, whether the accused is guilty or not guilty. Any German citizen without a criminal record can become a lay judge. See also p. 11.

plaintiff: a person in a civil case who has been injured or who feels they have suffered harm and who is suing the defendant. See also p. 11.

prosecutor: a lawyer whose job it is to try to prove in court that the accused committed a crime. See also p. 11.

regulation: an official rule made by a government.

sentence: a punishment that a criminal receives in court. See also p. 12.

shoplifting: the crime of stealing something from a shop by deliberately leaving without paying for it.

tax: money that you have to pay to the government so that it can pay for public services.

witness: a person who appears in court and gives evidence in the witness box. See also p. 11.

witness box: the place in court where people sit to give evidence.

Charts and diagrams

Cause-and-effect diagrams

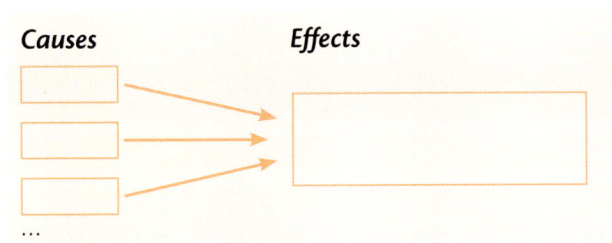

Flow chart

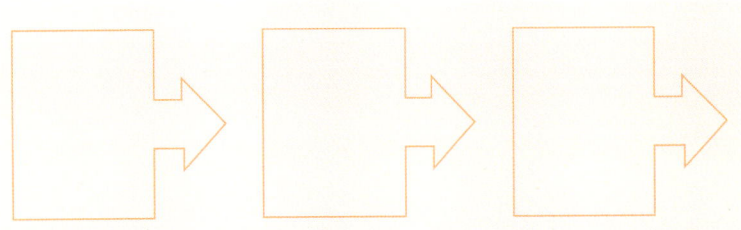

English-German vocabulary

A

accused [ə'kjuːzd] *Angeklagte/-r*

achieve an aim *ein Ziel erreichen*

affect sb./sth. *auf jdn./etwas auswirken*

air-pollution filter *Rußpartikelfilter*

allow sb. to do sth. *jdm. erlauben, etwas zu tun*

amount of *Menge an*

as a result of *aufgrund, infolge, zufolge*

B

ban (n) *Verbot*

ban sth. *etwas verbieten*

be able to afford sth. *sich etwas leisten können*

be allowed to do sth. [ə'laʊd] *etwas tun dürfen*

be in love with sb./sth. *sich in jdn./etwas verlieben*

be found guilty of sth. *einer Sache für schuldig befunden werden*

be involved in sth. *an etwas beteiligt sein*

because of sth. *wegen etwas*

break – broke – broken the law *gegen das Gesetz verstoßen*

by law *gesetzlich geregelt*

C

care instructions [ɪn'strʌkʃnz] *Pflegehinweis*

case *Prozess, Gerichtsverhandlung*

cause [kɔːz] *Ursache*

cause-and-effect diagram *Ursache-Wirkungs-Schema*

cereal ['sɪərɪəl] *Müsli*

charge (n) *Anklage*

charge sb. with sth. *jdn. einer Sache anklagen*

citizen ['sɪtɪzn] *Bürger/-in*

civil case *Zivilsache*

civil court *Zivilgericht*

claim sth. *etwas beanspruchen, fordern*

closing speech *Schlussplädoyer*

commit a crime *ein Verbrechen begehen*

common sense *gesunder Menschenverstand*

compensation *Schadenersatz, Entschädigung*

consequence ['kɒnsɪkwəns ☆ 'kɑːn-] *Auswirkung*

conviction *Urteil, Verurteilung*

copyright *Urheberrecht*

court [kɔːt] *Gericht*

court clerk [klɑːk ☆ klɜːrk] *Gerichtsdiener/in*

courtroom *Gerichtssaal*

create order *Ordnung schaffen*

crime *Verbrechen*

criminal case *Strafsache*

criminal court *Strafgericht*

D

damages (pl) *Schadenersatz*

damage sth. *etwas beschädigen*

decide on sth. *über etwas entscheiden*

decide sth. *sich für etwas entscheiden*

declare sb. guilty *jdn. für schuldig erklären*

declare sth. *etwas bekannt geben, etwas erklären*

defence counsel ['kaʊnsl] *Verteidiger/in*

defendant *Beklagte/-r*

demand sth. *etwas verlangen, fordern*

do the paper-round *Zeitungen austragen*

domestic [də'mestɪk] violence *häusliche Gewalt*

driving licence *Führerschein*

drop the charges *die Anklage fallenlassen*

E

effect *Wirkung, Auswirkung*

elect sb. *jdn. wählen*

enforce the law *das Gesetz durchsetzen*

even if *selbst wenn*

evidence *Beweis, Beweisstück*

experience *Erfahrung*

F

fake sth. *etwas fälschen*

file a complaint *eine Klageschrift einreichen*

file a police report against sb. *eine Anzeige gegen jdn. erstatten*

fine *Strafgebühr, Bußgeld*

flow chart *Flussdiagramm*

forbid sb. to do sth. *jdm. verbieten, etwas zu tun*

forbid sth. *etwas verbieten*

G

go free *freikommen*

guilty ['gɪlti] *schuldig*

H

harm sb./sth. *jdn./etwas verletzen, jdm. Schaden zufügen*

have a criminal record *vorbestraft sein*

have the effect that *die Auswirkung haben, dass*

household *Haushalt*

hurt sb./sth. *jdn./etwas verletzen*

I

influence ['ɪnfluəns] (n) *Einfluss*

injured party ['ɪndʒəd] *Geschädigte/-r*

investigation [ɪn,vestɪ'geɪʃn] *Untersuchung*

J

judge [dʒʌdʒ] *Richter/in*

justify sth. *etwas rechtfertigen*

L

law *Gesetz*

lawyer *Anwalt/Anwältin*

lay judge (r) *ehrenamtliche(r) Richter/in, Schöffe*

lead-led-led to sth. *führen zu etwas*

licence ['laɪsəns] *Lizenz*

M

money damages *Schadenersatz*

P

packaging (n) *Verpackung*
party *Partei*
pay a fine *eine Strafe bezahlen*
petrol *Benzin*
plaintiff ['pleɪntɪf] *Zivilkläger/-in*
plead guilty [pli:d] *sich schuldig bekennen*
police report *Polizeibericht*
property *Eigentum*
protect sb. from sth. *jdn. vor etwas schützen*
prove sth. [pru:v] *etwas beweisen*
public gallery *Zuschauergalerie*
public prosecutor *Staatsanwalt/-anwältin*
punish sb./sth. *jdn./etwas bestrafen*
punishment *Strafe*

Q

question sb. *jdn. verhören, befragen*

R

raise sth. *etwas erhöhen*
reason *Grund*
regulate sth. ['regjuleɪt] *etwas regulieren*
regulation *Regulation*
relative *Verwandte/-r*
remain silent *schweigen*
reported shoplifting cases *erfasste Ladendiebstähle*
represent sb./sth. *jdn./etwas vertreten*
representative *Vertreter/-in*
robe *Talar*
rule *Regel*

S

scratch sb./sth. *jdn./etwas zerkratzen*
search sth. *etwas durchsuchen*
sentence (n) *Verurteilung*
sentence sb. to sth. (v) *jdn. zu etwas verurteilen*
shoplifting *Ladendiebstahl*
solve sth. *etwas lösen*
speed (n) *Geschwindigkeit*
speed gun *Geschwindigkeitsmesser*
speeding (n) *Geschwindigkeitsüberschreitung*
state *feststellen, sagen*
sue [su:] sb. for sth. *jdn. wegen etwas verklagen, etwas von jdm. einklagen*
suffer *leiden*
suffer damages *Schaden erleiden*
suspect *Verdächtige/-r*
suspect sb. of sth. *jdn. einer Sache verdächtigen*
swear an oath [əʊθ ☆ oʊθ] *einen Eid ablegen*

T

tell the truth *die Wahrheit sagen*
test sth. *etwas prüfen*
The Protection of Young Persons Employment Act *Jugendarbeitsschutzgesetz*
traffic warden *Politesse*
treat sb./sth. unfairly *jdn./etwas ungerecht behandeln*
trial ['traɪəl] *Gerichtsverhandlung*
try – tried – tried sb. *jdn. vor Gericht stellen*

U

under oath [əʊθ ☆ oʊθ] *unter Eid*
unfairly *ungerecht*

V

verdict *Urteilsspruch, Gerichtsurteil*

W

witness *Zeuge/Zeugin*
witness box *Zeugenbank*

German-English vocabulary

A

Abschnitt *paragraph*
Aktion *action*
aktuell *current/topical*
Amateur- *amateur*
Angeklagte/-r *accused*
Angelegenheit *matter, issue*
jdn. einer Sache anklagen *charge sb. with sth.*
etwas ankündigen *announce sth.*
etwas anstecken *set sth. on fire*
Anstieg *increase, rise*
Anwalt/Anwältin *lawyer*
jdn. anzeigen *press charges against sb.*
auffallend *striking*
aufgrund *as a result of sth.*
Auswirkung auf jdn./etwas *effect on sb./sth.*
auf jdn./etwas auswirken *affect sb./sth.*

B

basiert auf etwas *based on sth.*
etwas beanspruchen *claim sth.*
jdn./etwas beeinflussen *affect sb./sth.*
ein Verbrechen begehen *commit a crime*
etwas bekannt geben *declare sth.*
sich schuldig bekennen *plead guilty*
Beklagte/-r *defendant*
Bekleidung *clothing*
Benzin *petrol*
etwas beschädigen *damage sth.*
etwas beschränken *limit sth.*
Beschreibung *description*
besonders *particularly*
Bestätigung *statement*
jdn./etwas bestrafen *punish sb./sth.*
etwas betrachten *consider sth.*
Betrieb *company, business*
etwas beweisen *prove sth.*
Beweis *evidence*
eine Strafe bezahlen *pay a fine*
bezüglich *concerning*
Bürger/-in *citizen*

D

daher *thus*
deutlich *noticeably*
Drogen *drugs*
etwas durchsuchen *search sth.*
etwas tun dürfen *be allowed to do sth.*

E

ehrenamtliche(r) Richter/-in *lay judge*
einen Eid ablegen *swear an oath*
unter Eid *under oath*
Eigentum *property*
man gewinnt/bekommt den Eindruck, dass *you get the impression that*
emotional *emotional*
Entschädigungssumme *money damages*
über etwas entscheiden *decide on sth.*
Ereignis *incident*
Erfahrung *experience*
etwas erhöhen *raise sth.*
jdm. erlauben, etwas zu tun *allow sb. to do sth.*
Erlaubnis *permission*
Schaden erleiden *suffer damages*
etwas erreichen *reach sth.*
Anzeige gegen jdn. erstatten *file a report against sb.*
etwas erwarten *expect sth.*
etwas entwerfen *design sth.*

F

Feld *field*
feststellen *state*
Feuerwehrmann *fireman*
Firma *business, company*
etwas fordern *demand sth.*
Führerschein *driving licence*
etwas fürchten *fear sth.*

G

Gefängnis *prison*
gegen das Gesetz verstoßen *break – broke – broken the law*
im Gegensatz zu jdm./etwas *in contrast to sb./sth.*
Geldstrafe *fine*
Gericht *court*
Gerichtsdiener/in *court clerk*
Gerichtssaal *courtroom*
Gerichtsverhandlung *trial*
Geschädigte/-r *injured party*
Geschäft *business*
Geschwindigkeitsüberschreitung *speeding*
Gesetz *law*
günstig, billig *cheap*

H

Haushalt *household*
häusliche Gewalt *domestic violence*
Helm *helmet*
etwas hervorbringen *bring about sth.*

I

jdn. informieren *inform sb.*
insbesondere *notably, in particular*

J

Jugendarbeitsschutzgesetz *The Protection of Young Persons Employment Act*

K

kaum *hardly, scarcely*
körperlich *physically*
Künstler/in *artist*

L

Ladendieb *shoplifter*
Ladendiebstahl *shoplifting*
leiden *suffer*
sich etwas leisten können *be able to afford sth.*
Lizenz *licence*
etwas lösen *solve sth.*

M

Mangel an etwas *lack of sth.*
Menge an *amount of*
gesunder Menschenverstand *common sense*
Minderjährige/-r *minor*
etwas missachten *violate sth.*
jdn./etwas misshandeln *treat sb./sth. unfairly*
Mülleimer *rubbish bin*

N

nach jdm./etwas *according to sb./sth.*
Nachbar/-in *neighbour*
nachsichtig *lenient*

O

obwohl *even though*
öffentlich sein *be public*
Öffentlichkeit *public (n)*

P

Phase *stage*
Polizeibericht *police report*
professionell *professional*
Prozess *court case*

R

rauchen *smoke (v)*
etwas rechtfertigen *justify sth.*
Regel *rule*
Regulation *regulation*
etwas regulieren *regulate sth.*
Reparaturen *repairs*
Resultate *findings*
Richter/-in *judge*
Rußpartikelfilter *air-pollution filter*

S

die Wahrheit sagen *tell the truth*
Schadenersatz *compensation*
Schlussfolgerung *conclusion*
Schlussplädoyer *closing speech*
schuldig *guilty*
jdn. vor etwas schützen *protect sb. from sth.*
schweigen *remain silent*
Staatsanwalt/-anwältin *public prosecutor*
Stehlen *stealing*
jdn. vor Gericht stellen *try sb.*
Steuer *tax*
Strafe *punishment*
Strafgericht *criminal court*
etwas streichen *paint sth.*
streiken *strike*
streng *strict*
Studienfach *subject*

T

täglich *daily*
Tätigkeit *activity*
Tatsache *fact*
teuer *expensive*

U

sich etwas überlegen *consider sth.*
jdn. überraschen *surprise sb.*
ungefähr *approximately, roughly*
Untersuchung *investigation*
Urheberrecht *copyright*
Ursache *cause*
Urteil, Verurteilung *conviction*

V

etwas verbieten *ban sth.*
jdm. verbieten, etwas zu tun *forbid sb. to do sth.*
Verbot *ban (n)*
Verbrechen *crime*
Verbrechensopfer *crime victim*
Verdächtige/-r *suspect*
vergleichbar *comparable, similar*
etwas vergleichen (mit etwas) *compare sth. (with sth.)*
jdn. verhören *question sb.*
jdn. wegen etwas verklagen *sue sb. for sth.*
etwas verlangen *demand sth.*
jdn./etwas verletzen *hurt, harm sb./sth.*
Verteidiger/-in *defence counsel*
jdn./etwas vertreten *represent sb./sth.*
Verurteilung *sentence (n)*
vorbestraft sein *have a criminal record*
sich etwas vorstellen *imagine sth.*

W

Wecker *alarm clock*
wegen etwas *because of sth.*
Wirkung, Auswirkung *effect*

Z

Zeitungen austragen *do the paper-round*
Zeuge/Zeugin *witness*
Zeugenbank *witness box*
Zivilgericht *civil court*
Zivilkläger/-in *plaintiff*
einer Sache / jdm. zustimmen *agree with sth./sb.*
jdm. etwas zuerkennen *award sth. to sb.*